I Love TO WORSHIP

Take Your Rightful Place

By
Diane Thompson

Illustrations By
Ke'Ron Hall

AuthorHouse™
1663 Liberty Drive
Bloomington, IN 47403
www.authorhouse.com
Phone: 1 (833) 262-8899

Because of the dynamic nature of the Internet, any web addresses or links contained in this book may have changed
since publication and may no longer be valid. The views expressed in this work are solely those of the author and do not
necessarily reflect the views of the publisher, and the publisher hereby disclaims any responsibility for them.

Any people depicted in stock imagery provided by Getty Images are models,
and such images are being used for illustrative purposes only.
Certain stock imagery © Getty Images.

This book is printed on acid-free paper.

NLT
Scripture quotations marked NLT are taken from the Holy Bible, New Living Translation, copyright © 1996, 2004, 2007.
Used by permission of Tyndale House Publishers, Inc. Carol Stream, Illinois 60188. All rights reserved. Website

ISBN: 978-1-6655-0120-0 (sc)
ISBN: 978-1-6655-0119-4 (e)

Library of Congress Control Number: 2020918608

Print information available on the last page.

Published by AuthorHouse 09/25/2020

authorHOUSE®

Special Thanks to:
God The Father, Son and Holy Spirit
Faith Mission Ministries: Apostle Harold K.
Browning and Prophet Gwen Browning
Nella Thompson, Nella Derrico, Derica Thompson,
Zariah Thompson, Derek Thompson

Hello boys and girls my name is Diane
and I love to worship God.
I worship God by flagging and dancing.

I worship and love God because God loves me.
God declares "For I know the plans I
have for you", "Plans to prosper
you and not to harm you, plans to
give you hope and a future".

When I worship God I worship from a Place
of Victory. God's word declares everyone
born of God overcomes the world.

Not only do I love to flag and dance but I also love to pray. God says "don't worry about anything but pray about everything. Tell God what you need, and thank him for all he has done".

I 'am A Royal Priesthood!
You are A Royal Priesthood too!

So let's worship together and Don't forget to pray.

Meet the Illustrator

Most importantly, Ke'Ron Hall is a Christian. Through faith and experience his gifts have made room for him to include freelancing as a creative and artist. His skillset encompasses graphic design, fashion design, photography, spoken word poetry, writing, illustrating and modeling. Originally born in Columbia, South Carolina, Hall moved to Tennessee in 2001 due to his family being stationed at Fort Campbell. While living in Clarksville, he acquired both a high school diploma in 2016 and an Associate's Degree from Austin Peay State University; he is currently pursuing a degree in computer science. His love for the creative arts stemmed from his young age and gradually developed throughout the years. He hopes to continue doing so to expand upon his passion and provide ministry to others as a young man of God.

Printed in the United States
By Bookmasters